ingan

IMPOSSIBLE

Handbook of Hatebusting

ABHIJIT NASKAR

Ingan Impossible: Handbook of Hatebusting

("Ingan/인간" is Korean for "Human")

Copyright © 2022 Abhijit Naskar

This is a work of non-fiction

An Amazon Publishing Company, 1st Edition, 2022

Printed in the United States of America

ISBN: 9798840734285

INGAN IMPOSSIBLE

Abhijit Naskar is the twenty-first century Neuroscientist whose contributions in Cognitive and Behavioral Neuroscience have helped the world tackle the issues of systemic racism, prejudice, hate, extremism, discrimination and biases more effectively. As an untiring advocate of mental health and universal acceptance, he became a beloved best-selling author all over the world with his very first book "The Art of Neuroscience in Everything". With his pioneering ventures into the Neuropsychology of beliefs and biases, he has hugely contributed in the eradication of religious and cultural differences in our world, for which he is popularly hailed as the humanitarian scientist, who takes the human civilization in the path of sweet general harmony.

Also by Abhijit Naskar

The Art of Neuroscience in Everything
Your Own Neuron: A Tour of Your Psychic Brain
The God Parasite: Revelation of Neuroscience
The Spirituality Engine
Love Sutra: The Neuroscientific Manual of Love
Homo: A Brief History of Consciousness
Neurosutra: The Abhijit Naskar Collection
Autobiography of God: Biopsy of A Cognitive Reality
Biopsy of Religions: Neuroanalysis towards Universal
Tolerance
Prescription: Treating India's Soul
What is Mind?
In Search of Divinity: Journey to The Kingdom of Conscience
Love, God & Neurons: Memoir of a scientist who found
himself by getting lost
The Islamophobic Civilization: Voyage of Acceptance
Neurons of Jesus: Mind of A Teacher, Spouse & Thinker
Neurons, Oxygen & Nanak
The Education Decree
Principia Humanitas
The Krishna Cancer
Rowdy Buddha: The First Sapiens
We Are All Black: A Treatise on Racism
The Bengal Tigress: A Treatise on Gender Equality
Either Civilized or Phobic: A Treatise on Homosexuality
Wise Mating: A Treatise on Monogamy
Illusion of Religion: A Treatise on Religious
Fundamentalism
The Film Testament
Human Making is Our Mission: A Treatise on Parenting
I Am The Thread: My Mission
7 Billion Gods: Humans Above All
Lord is My Sheep: Gospel of Human
Morality Absolute
A Push in Perception
Let The Poor Be Your God
Conscience over Nonsense
Saint of The Sapiens
Time to Save Medicine
Fabric of Humanity
Build Bridges not Walls: In the name of Americana
The Constitution of The United Peoples of Earth

Lives to Serve Before I Sleep
When Humans Unite: Making A World Without Borders
All For Acceptance
Monk Meets World
Mission Reality
Citizens of Peace: Beyond The Savagery of Sovereignty
Operation Justice: To Make A Society That Needs No Law
See No Gender
The Gospel of Technology
Every Generation Needs Caretakers: The Gospel of
Patriotism
Aşkanjali: The Sufi Sermon
Mad About Humans: World Maker's Almanac
Revolution Indomable
When Call The People: My World My Responsibility
No Foreigner Only Family
Hurricane Humans: Give me accountability, I'll give you
peace
Ain't Enough to Look Human
Servitude is Sanctitude
Time To End Democracy: The Meritocratic Manifesto
I Vicdansaadet Speaking: No Rest Till The World is Lifted
Boldly Comes Justice: Sentient not Silent
Good Scientist: When Science and Service Combine
Sleepless for Society
Neden Türk: The Gospel of Secularism
Martyr Meets World: To Solve The Hard Problem of
Inhumanity
The Shape of A Human: Our America Their America
When Veins Ignite: Either Integration or Degradation
Heart Force One: Need No Gun to Defend Society
Solo Standing on Guard: Life Before Law
Generation Corazon: Nationalism is Terrorism
Mucize Insan: When The World is Family
Hometown Human: To Live for Soil and Society
Girl Over God: The Novel (Abi Naskar Adventures Book 1)
Gente Mente Adelante: Prejudice Conquered is World
Conquered
Earthquakin' Egalitarian: I Die Everyday So Your Children
Can Live
Giants in Jeans: 100 Sonnets of United Earth
Vatican Virus: The Forbidden Fiction (Abi Naskar
Adventures Book 2)
Karadeniz Chronicle: The Novel (Abi Naskar Adventures

Book 3)
Şehit Sevda Society: Even in Death I Shall Live
Handcrafted Humanity: 100 Sonnets For A Blunderful
World
Mücadele Muhabbet: Gospel of An Unarmed Soldier
Making Britain Civilized: How to Gain Readmission to The
Human Race
Dervish Advaitam: Gospel of Sacred Feminines and Holy
Fathers
Honor He Wrote: 100 Sonnets For Humans Not Vegetables
The Gentalist: There's No Social Work, Only Family Work
Either Reformist or Terrorist: If You Are Terror I Am Your
Grandfather
Woman Over World: The Novel (Abi Naskar Adventures
Book 4)
High Voltage Habib: Gospel of Undoctrination
Bulldozer on Duty
Find A Cause Outside Yourself: Sermon of Sustainability

*This book is my response
to anti-asian hate.*

CONTENTS

1.   **Sapiens Impossible
(The Sonnet)**

Sapiens Impossible
(The Sonnet)

If my existence isn't impossible,
I do not wanna exist.
If my legacy isn't impossible,
I do not want to live.
If my breath doesn't breathe life,
I don't wanna take another breath.
If my veins don't invigorate another,
I have no need for such useless veins.
If my heart isn't proof of love impossible,
May this be the last time my heart beats.
If this being isn't the bridge of oneness,
May the bugs have a feast on some good eats.
I don't wanna live as a weakling of the jungle.
If I must live I'll live as sapiens impossible.

2. Hate is The Antithesis of Heart

Hate is the antithesis of heart. Hate is the antithesis of human. Therefore, it would be an understatement to say that, hate and human cannot coexist.

Yet the fact of the matter is - they do.

Which says a lot about the work that is yet to be done on ourselves.

But here's the thing.

Life creates problems based on its capacity for solution. My life is the question, my life is the answer. Thus speaks the human. Therefore, if the world is still infested with hate, it only means that we are not yet determined to treat it - heck, we are not even willing to recognize it as a problem!

In fact, in many cases, people take pride in their hate against the other. And that is a catastrophe. When hate becomes a matter of pride, then that's it - whether we live on earth or mars, we'll still be an uncivilized society.

We gotta have the will to be civilized - we gotta have the will to be human - we gotta have the will to be alive.

Hate is fear in action, abolish your fear and you'll abolish hate.

And we can never abolish our fear of each other so long as our mind is cluttered with filthy, barbaric beliefs of nationalism, cultural supremacy and so on. Hatelessness begins with sectlessness. World begins with nonsectarianism.

3. Müslümanım, Terörist Değil
(Dinim Şiiri – Turkish)

Müslümanım, Terörist Değil*
(Dinim Şiiri)

Evet, ben müslümanım, ama terörist değil,
Niye, her Amerikalı neonazi midir?
Nefret hayvanların niyetidir, ama,
Bir insanın niyeti aşk ve barıştır.
Benim için kimse kafir değil,
Çünkü, benim için merhamet inançtır.
Tanrı'ya inan, ya da inanma, farketmez,
Çünkü, sadece insanlıksız insan kafirdir.
Biz diyoruz su, onlar diyorlar water,
Ama su, susamış kişinin dinine bakmaz.
Benim için her iman gerçek ve eşittir,
Çünkü her şeyden önce biz insanız.
Hala nefret ediyorsan, senin nefretin sana mübarek.
Zor durumda olanlara yardım etmek, bir insanın ibadet.

(*This is the Turkish version of the sonnet
"Muslim Not Terrorist" from "Handcrafted Humanity:
100 Sonnets For A Blunderful World")

4. My Russia My Responsibility
(The Sonnet)

My Russia My Responsibility
(The Sonnet)

Moya Rossiya, moya lyubov, I am sorry,
That the world has turned its back on us.
But can you really blame them when,
We accepted a terrorist as a leader of ours!
Awake, arise, my brave comrades,
Drink deep from the valor of Volga.
I say, enough with apathy, for it is high time,
To sanitize our land against all domestic virus.
We let a terrorist loose on our neighbors,
And all that bloodshed is on our hands.
Even now if we don't mend our horrific error,
One savage will turn our world into a wasteland.
Mnogo te obicham, for you are still my home.
To humanize our home is the duty of none but our own.

5. Uproot All Exclusion

Unclutter the mind of all narcissistic jackassery, and this jackass world will finally begin to behave human. As I've said before, it's not enough to look human, we must behave human. We must be human - inside and out.

So, how do we do that?

How do we behave human?

We behave human by uprooting all desire for exclusion - by uprooting all exclusiveness - be it national, cultural, religious, political, ideological or any other.

For once, forget about the culture you are born in - forget about the nation you are born in - forget about the status you are born in - for once, forget all puny and pathetic prisons of narrowmindedness, and lose yourself in the vastness of humanity - lose yourself in others. For once, live, not to win anything, but to lose everything – every last trace of you.

Once you do - once you truly, genuinely, actually lose yourself in others all those societal prisons will have no appeal to you whatsoever, even if they are peddled by all your past ancestors and present relatives.

You know why?

Because one who loses themselves in others has the whole world as relative.

You see, the world doesn't need Avengers, the world needs Amantes. Hear me well my brave Amantes - it is time to assemble!

El mundo no necesita avengers, el mundo necesita amantes. Escúchenme bien, amantes - es hora de ensamblar. It is to assemble in love, rather than disassemble in hate.

6.   Amantes Assemble

By some sheer serendipity you've been endowed with several decades of existence as the most sentient being in the known universe.

Don't waste it on puny squabbles, my friend!

To climb the Everest is easy, to climb the heart is not so much. Yet it's the heart that is nearer to us than any other peak in the world. Climb the peak that is inside, and you won't have any need to climb any other peak.

To trek a heart is equivalent of trekking a thousand mountains. Trek yourself, climb yourself, conquer yourself. Keep on climbing, till you are unselfed!

Unselfed meaning?

Self beyond the self.

Can you take the self beyond the self? That is the question. Can you turn your exclusive self into an inclusive self - into an expansive self? And it is not really a question of whether you can, the real question is, do you want to?

If you do, from the very core of your being, that very want makes way for the emergence of an expansive self, drawing the strength of love and light from the untapped potential of the human heart. It is all about will.

The human world is a manifestation of the human will. **As you will, so will be.** You see, in reality, there is no handbook of hatebusting.

You know why? Because you are the handbook. You are the handbook of everything good and civilized that could ever happen to this world.

At the same time you are the handbook of all the destruction in the world.

So in the end, you have to decide - will you continue to live as a handbook of destruction like most of our ancestors did, or will you break that cycle and emerge as one of the very first handbooks of love, harmony and light!

You know what light means? Light means love, light means insight, light means gentleness, light means humility, and last but not the least, light means tenacity. And all these do not come from anywhere else, for they are all born of the human mind. They are all born of you.

7. Ain't The Center
    (The Sonnet)

Ain't The Center
(The Sonnet)

You are the Alpha,
You are Omega.
You are Altair,
You are the Vega.
You are the distance,
You are the contact.
You are the runner,
You are the racetrack.
You are the race,
You are the prize.
You are torchbearer,
You are the light.
You ain't the center of the universe.
For in reality, you are the universe.

8.   Not The Center of The Universe

You are not the center of the universe, you are the universe. In this human universe all divisions are born of the human, so is any possibility of unification. In this human universe darkness is born of the mind, so is light.

You just will it, my friend!

Will the light, will the might, will the sight, and you'll have flight.

Every atom within the human brain is teeming with light. Yet you know why it doesn't come to the surface? Because tradition and ignorance have conditioned the mind to labor more on raising walls rather than bringing them down.

Raising walls is an evolutionary trait, sure - but it is high time that we tell nature that we no longer have any need for such trait. And unlike other animal species, we humans have the brain capacity to take that decision.

Heck, if we didn't, we wouldn't even be considering the fact that something might be wrong about the way we've been behaving all this time. If we didn't have the brain capacity for expansion, we wouldn't even be considering the fact that something might be wrong about a trait that has been intrinsic to humankind's evolutionary history – a trait that has been instrumental to the survival of humankind in the jungle.

Let me put it to you this way. The capacity to question ourselves is a superpower. The capacity to correct ourselves is a superpower. To keep such potential stomped by bigotry and narcissism is the greatest tragedy of all.

9. All in The Mind
(The Sonnet)

All in The Mind
(The Sonnet)

Mind makes it dark,
Mind makes it bright.
Mind makes us weak,
Mind gives us might.
Mind makes us blind,
Mind gives us sight.
Mind makes us scared,
Mind gives us flight.
Mind makes us greedy,
Mind instills charity.
Mind raises the walls,
Mind wills all unity.
Mind is servant, mind is master.
Once truly aware, mind is hatebuster.

10. No Paradise Only People

38

Mind your mind before you mind the world, and in time the world will have all the right mind it needs – in time the world will have all the correction it needs. Realize the limitless expanse of your mind and in time the world will have all the rejuvenation it needs.

The world has borders because the mind has borders. The world has distance because the mind is distant. The world has discrimination because the mind thrives on discrimination. In fact, the mind is founded on discrimination.

What this means is that we are neurologically far more inclined to behave discriminatory than egalitarian and accepting. Yet it is on the foundation of acceptance and egalitarianism that we shall build a civilized world free from disparity and division.

And this can only happen when we take full reins of our society, as civilized humans are supposed to, despite our internal predispositions of inhumanity.

Remember, there is no heaven, only good human. There is no paradise, only good people. And the interesting part is that, anybody can be good and tender with people from similar background. This is no goodness - this is no tenderness – particularly when it's guided by tribalism instead of humanity.

Real goodness lies beyond background - real goodness lies beyond the fictitious borders of nation, culture, faith and everything remotely sectarian.

11. One Culture Ain't Enough

Would-be writers often ask me, do I ever get writer's block! I tell them, you get writer's block when you're imprisoned in one language and culture. Like the wind, I think, feel and live in numerous languages and cultures, which keeps me ever-ripe with more ideas than I could put down on pages.

Whether you are a writer or not, learn a language - it not only expands your head, it expands your heart, and makes you more humane. Porque, un idioma es una autopista a una cultura. A language is a freeway to a culture. Thus, learning a language is one of the tangible endeavors to help eliminate hate from the world.

You don't have to speak like a native - speak broken. Just the fact that you are willing to learn another language to get closer to another people makes you a vessel for assimilation - just the fact that you are willing to go beyond your habitual bounds makes you a force for expansive humanity.

And that's the whole point. Do you have the will to go beyond the bounds of the puny, sectarian identity imposed on you by your environment?

As I have said before. Culture should be a path, not a prison. And this is not just true for culture, but every single form of sectarianism there is. Nothing should be a prison.

As a matter of fact, anything that is dumped on you as a prison must be discarded at once - be it faith, state, status, ideology or anything else. Learn from everything and everybody, but be imprisoned by nothing and nobody.

12. Poet of A Planet
(The Sonnet)

46

Poet of A Planet
(The Sonnet)

I am not the poet of a nation,
I am the poet of a planet.
I don't do just one culture,
Assimilation is the prime tenet.
Hence my work repels nationalists,
Like the sun repels the nightcrawlers,
While it attracts expanding beings,
Like the amazon attracts explorers.
If you wanna hear how great your culture is,
Go read some fundamentalist fiction.
I don't write for prehistoric barbarians,
To put it bluntly, I write for modern humans.
I repeat, I'm not the poet of a single nation.
I am but the living proof of amalgamation.

48

13. No Slave to Culture
(The Sonnet)

No Slave to Culture
(The Sonnet)

What do you take me for - a street dog!
Slave to one religion, one nation, one culture!
Dinosaur here - wherever I lay my eyes,
Becomes my nation, my religion, my culture!
To add nationality to my name is to vilify my name,
Sectarianism and nonsectarianism don't go together.
To add exclusive ethnicity to my work is a violation,
Barbarism can't define the spirit of a human sonneteer.
Days of single nationality, single religion are gone,
It's the age of universal nationality and religion.
In this civilized age, human nationality is humanity,
Human religion and culture are love and compassion.
Exclusive ethnicity is a sign of a backward society.
Expand across the one imposed, and there'll be harmony.

14. Definition of Life

54

Religious fundamentalists often say, you don't need money, you don't need talent, you don't need status, you don't need anything except your faith in God.

Allow me to decode what this means.

It just means that the church has no need for a sentient human, it just needs a doormat for their dogmas. This, my friend, is anything but religion - it is the greatest blasphemy of all.

I'll say it plainly. Expansion is religion, narrowness is blasphemy. Reason is religion, prejudice is blasphemy. Curiosity is religion, belief without question is blasphemy.

The point is, each generation must write their own definition of religion - each generation must write their own definition of righteousness - each generation must write their own definition of proper human living.

In short, each new generation must carve their own definition of life. Each generation must figure out for themselves what life for their generation means. No generation must be asked to imprison themselves to the beliefs and habits of their ancestors.

Life lies in expansion, whereas stagnation only breeds death and disease. So, never imprison yourself, my friend!

But mind you, here some may think the opposite of imprisonment is absolute freedom.

So let me correct it. A society of absolute freedom is nothing but a fancy jungle, that is, with fancy exterior but a primitive interior. Absolute freedom is as dangerous as absolute obedience.

15. Discipline and Self-Regulation

You must have some discipline. Or else, you'll bring down the same doom upon yourself as our ancestors did with their primeval rigidity. Nobody is to discipline your life. But you must learn to discipline yourself.

But again I am not talking about a strict and rather heartless discipline. I am talking about a just and self-aware discipline - where you are aware of the lines that serve in the best interest of not just your own uplift, but also that of the society.

If you don't like the word discipline, let's just call it self-regulation. Don't let others regulate you, but you must learn to regulate yourself.

You must learn what freedom means and the responsibility that goes along with it, before you fall head over heels for the concept like a love-sick puppy.

You see, before freedom, must come accountability. Accountability earns its own freedom, and knows how to regulate it, whereas freedom without accountability only ruins the life of a person as well as an entire society.

The point is, humanity should drive the act of self-regulation, not rigidity and prejudice. What's needed is an expansive mind. A rigid mind sees the world in black and white, whereas an expansive mind recognizes the grey regions and acts accordingly - they act according to the best interest of not the self separate from the collective but the self as a reflection of the collective.

The world is your reflection, you are the world's reflection. The day you feel it in your bones, that day, my friend, you'll know what's right, what's wrong - that day you'll know what's human, what's inhuman - that day you'll know what is sense, what is nonsense.

And remember, do no pay much attention to the ridicule, as well as the admiration. Nobody will be there for you in the making, but everybody will be there in the taking. So never mind that.

What matters is your purpose. What matters is your work. What matters is your purposeful work - what matters is your workful purpose. Everything else is inconsequential - ridicule as well as admiration.

16. Use of A Ridicule

Care not about ridicule, care not about admiration, care only about love, light and life. I am not saying that you won't be bothered, you sure will - for if you are not bothered you ain't alive.

So what I am asking is this.

Let the admiration and mockery come and go. Do not indulge in either of them, beyond necessity, that is.

Now here's an interesting question. Admiration may feel necessary at times, but how could mockery and ridicule be necessary!

So let me elaborate. Sometimes the harshest ridicule holds the direst question - question that is necessary for self-correction – question that is necessary for self-improvement.

So although you must not take the ridicule to heart, always be aware of their possible potential to help you grow. For example, a great portion of my work is born as a response to ridicule.

That is why, I do not retaliate ridicule right away. Why let a good ridicule go to waste! Use it to your advantage. That's the wisest retaliation of ridicule there is.

A good ridicule fills my head with all sorts of ideas. In short, all the hate that I receive on a daily basis ends up being my aid rather than obstruction. No ridicule can be obstruction unless you allow it.

But mark you, I am not asking you to keep quiet in the face of hate, but you gotta learn when to blow your top, and when to keep your lid on.

It is impossible for me to take into account every single circumstance that you may face in life. To assume otherwise, would be a blasphemy on my part as well as yours. Who the hell am I to give you the full definition of your life!

Hear me well, my friend. It is your life, you may hold my hand occasionally, but the only person to guide you through your life, is you.

Life is to be its own guide. Mind is to be its own light. The pedestrian is to build their own path. Dream the path, be the path, live the path.

17. Action and Intent

You build a house with bricks and cement. You build a life with action and intent. You build a society with action and intent. Actions are the bricks and intent is the cement.

Action matters, intent matters. Let me tell you why. You see, our virtues may not be as deep-seated as our vices for evolutionary reason, but if we nourish our virtues and starve our vices long enough, in time, our virtues will be victorious.

But instead of doing that, if we give in to our vices for they come more naturally to us, then we only sustain a world with concrete on the outside and jungle on the inside.

So what is the way?

Fall in love – that's the way.

Fall in love beyond logic, beyond belief, and love will show the way. There is no place for conquest. There is no place for competition. There is no place for domination. Only place there is, is the place of love - only world there is, is the world of love.

I came, I saw, I lost myself - I lost myself in love with the people of this world. I know, the statement is not supposed to go this way. But guess what! Adages born of conquest and war do not suit a civilized society.

So, if someone thinks a statement is popular so it must be profound, they are dumber than a dumbbell. Just because something is popular doesn't make it great. Just because someone is popular doesn't make them a sage.

18. The Language You Can't Learn

Love is simple, yet there is nothing more profound than love. Love is easy, yet there is nothing more complicated than love. You know why it is like this? Because we try to fathom love, like we fathom everything else in this world - by the measure of self-centricity.

This won't do. It may work in all other walks of life, but such an attitude won't work in the domain of love. For in the domain of love, only language that makes any sense is love - not intellect, not belief, not doctrine, not compulsion of any kind – but love, and love alone.

And the most intriguing aspect of this language of love is that, it is not something you learn. All other languages you learn, but as to the language of love, you live.

You see what you know. What you don't know, you don't see, even if it is right in front of your eyes. Open your eyes my friend, not just those of your head, but also, more importantly, those of your heart.

Head open and heart open we'll escape the smog of segregation and supremacy. Once we do, we shall realize, la vida sin diversidad es humano sin humanidad. Life without diversity is human without humanity.

72

19. You Are More Than A Nationality

74

Tu mano en mi mano, nos haremos humano. Your hand in my hand we'll make the human hand. Your sight in my sight we shall develop foresight. Your step by my step we shall climb the Everest.

When we are together we are bulldozer. When we are divided we are the living dead. Togetherness breeds tomorrow. No togetherness no tomorrow.

Which means that oneness is not an option - oneness is necessity. Oneness is not a philosophy, it is the bedrock of humanity.

Community, community, community - that's what it all boils down to - not your community and my community, but one community - one humanity.

Humanity and community are the one and the same. We don't see it because in our mind community means something sectarian, something exclusive, something tribal.

We gotta eliminate this very sectarian tendency from our mind. We gotta eliminate this sense of exclusiveness from our mind. I am not asking you to erase all aspects of your cultural identity, for that would be yet another violation of human rights.

Rather what I am asking is that, do not think for a second that that's all you are - a mouthpiece for your culture - a showpiece from your culture. You are a living, breathing human being. And a being that doesn't expand is anything but human.

Your culture is a part of you, a very small part at that - it's not the whole of you. You are much more than a culture - you are much more than a faith - you are much more than a nationality.

20. World is My Family
(The Sonnet)

World is My Family
(The Sonnet)

Family is the world to everybody,
But to me the world is my family.
In the life of a true human,
Raising a wall is but blasphemy.
If the world is Juliet, I'm her Romeo,
If the world is Romeo, I'm his Juliet.
Amidst the storms of hate and hurt,
I am but an anchor of love and lenience.
I'll hide the world in my heart if necessary,
To provide sanctuary is the heart's purpose.
The struggle of this human will continue,
Till all drives of hate are memories of the past.
So I say again, my world is my responsibility.
Beware my dear bigots, I'm injurious to inhumanity!

21. Tüm Dünya Ailemdir
(Küresel Vatandaş Şiiri - Turkish)

Tüm Dünya Ailemdır*
(Küresel Vatandaş Şiiri)

Herkes için ailesi dünyadır
Ama benim için tüm dünya ailemdır.
Çünkü bir gerçek insanın hayatında,
Her duvar sadece kötü bir bedduadır.
Dünya Leyla ise ben sarhoş Mecnunum,
Eğer dünya mecnunsa ben leylayım.
Nefret fırtınalarının ortasında,
Ben sadece aşkın çapasıyım.
Gerekirse dünyayı kalbimde saklayacağım,
Kalbin amacı evsizler için bir ev olmaktır.
Mücadele edeceğim, savaşacağım, ama,
Ailemi bırakmayacağım son nefesime kadar.
Tekrar diyorum, dünya benim sorumluluk benim.
Bağnazlar dikkat, sağlığına çok zararlıyım.

(*This is the original Turkish version of
the sonnet "World is My Family")

22. Mental Piece
(The Sonnet)

Mental Piece
(The Sonnet)

In the west you call me humanitarian scientist,
Somewhere in the middle you call me pragmatist.
In the middle-east you call me sufi or dervish,
In the east you call me advaitin or nondualist.
No matter how you see me, you all are my own,
Each of you is family, each of you is my home.
Then there are those who ardently call me fraud,
Which also is a sign of love, but yet unknown.
I am not a person, prison or path, for I am vicdan,
I'm saadet, my friend, I am the spirit of unification.
Call the sun as you like, it still brightens the world,
In the domain of realization, to label is desecration.
All labels are equally right yet equally incomplete.
In a world full of showpiece I am but a mental piece.

23. Expansion Incarnate

You know what you are? You are expansion incarnate. A human being ought to be the proof of expansion, yet most spend their life being the dead carcass of a lifeless label.

This won't do. No matter how our ancestors lived their life, it won't do for us. If deep down the lifestyle of suits is the same as the lifestyle of brutes, then what's the point of all the suits in the first place!

Let me elaborate.

You know why there is so much economic disparity in the world?

Because the very concept of economy is founded on greed and alienation.

Think about this. After so many years of industrializing, in this so called advanced world, we haven't yet succeeded in ensuring the access to fundamentals of life for everyone across status.

On the contrary, we've made it a point to focus on the fact that, if you have no status you are bound to die of starvation on the streets, and nobody is going to be responsible for your suffering.

But guess what! Somebody is responsible - for someone's lack of access to the essentials of life.

Who you ask?

Each and every person who indulges in luxury beyond necessity, without having any concern for collective uplift, is responsible for someone else's lack of access to the fundamentals of life – they are responsible for all the disparities in the world – not the billionaires, but these so-called commoners with greed bigger than the great Khali's hug.

24. Financial Freedom
(The Sonnet)

Financial Freedom
(The Sonnet)

Financial freedom doesn't mean,
To be free from money troubles.
Financial freedom actually means,
Freedom from obsession of dollar bills.
When the mind learns to distinguish,
Between luxury and actual necessity.
That's the beginning of financial freedom,
That's the beginning of economic stability.
Modern economy is the antithesis of sustainability,
Where financial freedom is bait to the suckers.
Actual necessities of life are very little,
But first you gotta break free from the predators.
We gotta wake up from materialism to be free.
Or else, scheme after scheme we'll be ever unfree.

25. Ride A Bike (The Sonnet)

Ride A Bike
(The Sonnet)

Ride a bike 'n you get sick less,
You pay for the doctor less.
Ride a bike 'n you emit carbon less,
You pay for the gas less.
Ride a bike 'n you release endorphins,
Hence you have less stress.
Ride a bike 'n the heart pumps better,
Thus you feel exhaustion less.
Pills in need are pills indeed,
To pop pills willy-nilly is to abuse health.
Comfort in need is comfort indeed,
To abuse comfort beyond need is to abuse oneself.
Ride a bike everyday to keep the pills away.
Use pills in need but don't make them life's way.

26. Disparity, Education and Economy

Every dollar spent on luxury is a dollar of disparity. Citizens of earth could force big tech to pay their employees fair wages tomorrow, if they just stop buying their fancy, overpriced products and go for humbler alternatives unless the companies bring down their disparities in salary.

The CEO may enjoy certain benefits of their position, but not until those working at the bottom can afford the fundamentals of life for their family. I'll say it to you plainly. An employee wronged is a company wronged.

You see, trying to build a disparity-free economy pursuing revenue is like trying to achieve pregnancy through vasectomy. So long as greed drives the economy, it's not economy, but catastrophe. So long as greed drives the industries, it's not industrialization, it is vandalization.

Ambition to climb the ladder of status so that you could be on the affluent side of disparity, is no ambition of a civilized human, it's the ambition of a caveman. So, before you pursue an ambition in life, educate yourself on a civilized definition of ambition.

Yet the situation in our world is so pathetic that that's exactly the kind of ambition educational institutes sell. Schools and universities don't teach you to build a civilized society free from disparity, they teach you clever tactics to be on the affluent side of disparity. This is not education, this is castration.

Concern for the society should be the bedrock of education - collective welfare should be the bedrock of economy - if not, we might as well start living as hobos on the streets, because with greed as the driving principle of education and economy, sooner or later all of us will end up on the streets.

27. Information isn't Education

So what do we do?

What else – we gotta educate ourselves - and I mean really educate ourselves - not by reading a lot of books, but by asking a ton of questions.

Books are a part of learning, but they are not the whole of learning. Real learning takes place in the being, not in books.

Information isn't education. Information comes from outside, education comes from inside. Absorb the information from the outside, then look for the answer inside.

And believe you me, if you look naively enough, if you look intently, if you look bravely enough, you'll find the answer - no matter the question, you'll find the answer.

You know how I know this! Because all the problems of the human society are born of the human mind. And what one mind can ruin, another mind can fix. The fixing itself is not the problem, the real question is how badly do you want to fix the world!

You see, messiahs don't fall from the sky. A messiah is a mortal, minus the indifference. And indifference disappears when intent appears - intent appears when love appears.

108

28. What is The World to You

What it boils down to is this. Do you love this world? Do you love the people of this world? Do you love the people of this world as your family - not more or less, but exactly as your family?

What is this world to you? What are its people to you? What is this society to you?

I don't know the answer. Do you?

The world must find its way. And for that the individual must find their way. The individual must find their answer.

So go - go down to the dust and dirt of the streets and the soil, and find your answer. Your own heart holds the answer, sure. But if the streets and the soil don't squeeze the answer out of you, nothing can, no one can.

You won't find the answer to life cooped up on your couch of comfort – on your couch of convenience, both material and mental. You gotta embrace the inconvenience of the world - you gotta embrace the chaos of the world. Once you do - once you absorb the entire world through every pore of you being, answer will come on its own - order will come on its own.

Order is nothing but a friendship with chaos. And answer is born of the friendship with question. Run from chaos and you'll never find order. Run from the questions and you'll never find the answer.

Besides, how far are you going to run?

Sooner or later chaos catches up. Sooner or later the questions catch up.

Nobody can hide forever. Sooner or later you gotta face the music - unless you come up with your own original music.

29. It's 21st Century AD, Not BC

Be the music my friend - the world has too much noise - be the music. A noisy world ends up filling your head with noise - unless your head is already saturated with an indefatigable and exuberant music of its own.

Do you have such music of your own in your head? Do you have such music of your own in your heart?

If you do, then what are you waiting for! Play it.

If you don't, then what are you waiting for! Make it.

Your music will offend many. It's okay. Don't cuss them like they do. Don't hate them like they do. You just do you and make your music - you just be you and play your music.

Remember, lines drawn by savages are bound to be crossed by thinking humans. If we don't, out of fear of persecution, then we shall never see the light of civilization.

After all, we can't live in the 21st century AD pretending it's 21st century BC. Just like we can't live in the 41st century AD pretending it's 21st century AD - if we survive that long that is.

Let me put this into perspective. You can't expect the people of the 41st century to find answers to all their questions of life in my works. They may find some, but not all. Just like that, you can't expect to find the answers to the questions of life of today in literature written thousands of years ago.

Literature helps, sure, but no literature is absolute, no literature is complete - not mine, or anybody else's.

I am not the answer to your life, you are. I may be the trigger, but you yourself are the answer. You are your own question. You are your own answer.

30. To See Color (The Sonnet)

To See Color
(The Sonnet)

The problem is not that you see color,
It is that you assume character from color.
The problem is not that you see gender,
It is that you assume capacity from gender.
The problem is not that you see religion,
It is that you assume tendency from religion.
The problem is not that you see profession,
It is that you assume worth from profession.
The problem is not that you see sexuality,
It is that you assume nature from sexuality.
The problem is not that you see nationality,
It is that you assume honor from nationality.
The main problem is not that you make assumptions.
It is that you assume yourself beyond examination.

31. This is How We Make All Lives Matter (The Sonnet)

This is how we make
all lives matter
(The Sonnet)

Wherever a black life is shot of suspicion,
I am that black life that didn't matter.
Wherever a woman is forced to remain pregnant,
I am that woman who doesn't matter.
Wherever a muslim is presumed terrorist,
I am that muslim who doesn't matter.
Wherever a queer life is persecuted,
I am that queer who doesn't matter.
Standing up to cannibalism requires,
No exclusive background and identity.
All that matters is that you are human,
Only requirement of justice is humanity.
This is how we make all lives matter, all lives free.
Injustice on anyone anywhere is injustice on me.

32. Motherless Motherhood
(The Sonnet)

Motherless Motherhood
(The Sonnet)

To take choice out of pregnancy,
Is to take the mother out of motherhood.
If childbirth isn't the mother's will,
Who the hell is state to make the rule!
State is a servant of the people,
Church is a servant of the people.
When they claim to be guardian supreme,
People must stand to spoil their gamble.
To take choice out of democracy,
Is to take citizens out of government.
But to take bigotry out of politics,
Is to take politics out of the state.
A society that equates woman with womb,
Is a society headed for its own tomb.

128

33. There is Not One Society

Society starts with you, society ends with you. But we must investigate a little further into the nature of this so-called concept of society. It's imperative.

There is not really much to say about it that I haven't said already in my other works, except for this.

There is not one, but two society. One is snobbish, narcissistic and judgmental to the bone. Another is too hungry to judge anyone. If we must serve, let us be servant to the society that nobody cares about, and to hell with the society that everybody tries to impress and wants to be a part of.

Lick the boots of those in the lap of luxury and you'll only end up as fodder for disparity. But lift up those who are fallen, even at the expense of your own security, and the entire world will be bestowed with equality.

Equalization and revenue generation are not the same thing. Sometimes to equalize the society we may have to take a beating in the revenue department, whereas often times generation of revenue involves horrendous violations of human rights. This isn't economics, this is humanity 101.

For example, if I keep the titles of my works strictly in English, it would reflect positively on my sales. But I don't do that. You know why? Because that would defeat the very purpose of my work.

Besides, I cannot even produce any work unless I feel the title. So I have to use the titles as they appear to me. And in case you are wondering, how I know whether a title is right for a particular work, the answer is this.

As I have said many a times, I have no control over my words, including the titles. Every time a title appears in my mind it sends a chill down my spine. The entire body shakes up in momentary tremor followed by the rush of an immense tranquility. And that's it! Right or not, that is the title.

The same happens whenever I come up with a radical statement. Just like Ramanujan used to have visions of numbers, I have visions of words, that too, in the most socially relevant manner possible. I wish I could claim credit for them, but the fact of the matter is, I have no control over these visions.

Not all my works are born this way, but if there is any particular statement of mine that appeals to you the most, chances are, it is born of a vision. However, do not go thinking of it as some sort of mystical phenomenon. All these so-called mystical phenomena have very natural roots, which I elaborated quite in detail in my early works.

34. Elitism & Fundamentalism
(The Sonnet)

Elitism & Fundamentalism
(The Sonnet)

Elitism and fundamentalism,
Are both the enemies of progress.
Exchanging one bad habit for another,
Is not true advancement but regress.
Fundamentalists used to fill the world,
With the poison of dirty division.
Today elitists poison the world,
By endorsing snobbery and narcissism.
Conscience, courage and compassion,
These are the three pillars of progress.
Without these all belief is delusion,
All glitter is but a sign of coldness.
Replace not fundamentalism with elitism.
Grow out of selfishness into collectivism.

35. Do You Know Who I Am
(The Sonnet)

Do you know who I am
(The Sonnet)

Oh, so many times have I heard,
Do you know who I am!
So today when I travel places,
I walk around as a total lamb!
There's an immense relief,
In not flashing my name.
Windbags make all the noise,
Beings with character stay inane.
Be an elephant, strong yet gentle,
You observe more by being a dumbbell.
Blow your top when it's really needed,
Otherwise, be good people among the people.
All roads lead to people, not to mythical Rome.
Names aloof from people have no living role.

36. Make A Name
(The Sonnet)

Make A Name
(The Sonnet)

Make a name to give hope,
Not to have control over people.
Make a name to lift another,
Not to look down on the people.
Be a symbol that burns bright,
Even when you are not around.
Selfish self is septic self,
Be an epitome of sacrifice unbound.
Only fools dream of ruling the world,
Sapiens dream of self-annihilation.
I dream, breathe and live as servant,
Servanthood brings sanctification.
Fall without fail at the feet of the forgotten.
Lend a hand to lift a heart, together we are beacon.

37. Politics is The New Opium
(The Sonnet)

Politics is The New Opium
(The Sonnet)

I started writing on politics to impress a girl,
Then she left for a native white, balkan alternative.
But I was too deep in the pickle to leave politics,
Eventually the struggling nobody arose a global native.
Originally I was inclined towards writing on religion,
But soon I realized justice is the religion of tomorrow.
And the world's notion of religion is beyond repair,
Terms of religion lost their charm to me more and more.
Religion was the opium for the masses of yesterday,
Politics is opium for the masses of today.
But politics of pop culture is not what I work on,
My politics is not left or right, but mostly grey.
As a brain scientist, my work is to dissect human nature.
If it makes way for a better society, that's a great honor.

38. Responsibility Brings Greatness

The point is, sometimes to practice humanity one has to make some monetary compromise. Right or not, it is the human thing to do. The same holds true for a company as well as a society.

Now the question is, knowing all this, how will you proceed further?

The answer will be apparent to you only when you have your priorities straight. And I mean the right answer will be apparent to you only when you have your priorities straight as a living, breathing human being.

It all comes down to a simple sense of responsibility towards others - those who are strangers - those who may look different - those who may speak different - those who have no relation of blood with you whatsoever.

Let me put it to you another way. I am not an extraordinary scientist. I have no desire to be one. But I'll tell you this. An average scientist with an extraordinary sense of responsibility towards society does more good to the world than an extraordinary scientist with a lousy sense of responsibility.

Responsibility brings greatness, not intellect. Accountability makes one human, not appearance. Behavior makes one sapient, not background. Only the barbarians care about background. Humans take the ground and make it their background.

39. Social Reform 101
(The Sonnet)

Social Reform 101
(The Sonnet)

Brute force isn't always the answer,
Sometimes you gotta be clever.
Naivety has its place, it keeps you humble,
Dealing with hyenas you gotta be a dinosaur.
I am not talking about size and appearance,
Appearance never brings any lasting change.
Here I am talking about the faculties within,
For corruption is defeated only by a hearty brain.
The best way to control the manipulator is,
To give them the illusion of control 'n dominance.
To con the con-artist for the greater good,
Is not an act of con but an act of conscience.
Sentiment is good, but without wisdom it is plain stupid.
An activist fights the system, a reformer manipulates it.

40. Ground is Background

Stand on the ground. Do not take a high and mighty pedestal, aloof from everyday life, take the lowest ground and work from there. Work the ground and the ground will work on you - that is, the more you work on the ground the more you work on yourself - thus you become less animal and more human with every single act.

So my friend, I say again.

Leave the pedestals for the stuffed animals. You for one, take the ground. Take the ground, work the ground, live the ground, and lift the ground. There is no other way. Ground is the only way. Soil is the only way. Soil is the highway.

If we are to erase hate from the world, we can do that only by working in the soil, on the streets. If we are to erase inhumanity from the world, we can do that only by toiling in the soil and on the streets.

Libraries, capitol buildings, all are okay, but that's not where change comes from. Spend some time at the library if you so desire, spend some time at the capitol building if you so desire, but sooner or later, you must come down to the streets.

Because contrary to popular belief, government buildings and educational institutes are not the nerve centers of society - the true nerve centers of society are the streets - streets that bear witness to the struggles of life - streets that bear witness to the labor of liberty - streets that bear witness to the struggles of being treated as an equal member of the human family.

BIBLIOGRAPHY

Archer M., (2000), Being Human: The Problem of Agency. Cambridge University Press.

Adolphs R (2003) Cognitive neuroscience of human social behaviour. Nature Rev Neurosci 4: 165–178.

Adolphs R, Tranel D, Damasio AR (2003) Dissociable neural systems for recognizing emotions. Brain Cogn 52: 61–69.

Andresen, Jensine, and Robert Forman, eds. Cognitive Models and Spiritual Maps. Bowling Green, Ohio: Imprint Academic, 2000.

Azari, Nina, Janpeter Nickel, Gilbert Wunderlich, Michael Niedeggen, Harald Hefter, Lutz Tellmann, Hans Herzog, Petra Stoerig, Dieter Birnbacher, and Rudiger Seitz. "Neural Correlates of Religious Experience."

European Journal of Neuroscience 13, no. 8 (2001)

Agar, N. (2004). Liberal eugenics: In defence of human enhancement. London: Blackwell Publishing.

Alteheld, N., Roessler, G., Vobig, M., & Walter, R. (2004). The retina implant new approach to a visual prosthesis. Biomedizinische Technik, 49(4), 99–103.

Antal, A., Nitsche, M. A., Kincses, T. Z., Kruse, W., Hoffmann, K. P., & Paulus, W. (2004a). Facilitation of visuo-motor learning by transcranial direct current stimulation of the motor and extrastriate visual areas in humans. European Journal of Neuroscience, 19(10), 2888–2892.

Bernstein R.J., (1971), Praxis and Action: Contemporary Philosophies of Human Activity. Philadelphia: University of Pennsylvania Press.

Bernstein R.J., (1976), The Restructuring Social and Political Thought.

Bernstein R.J., (1983), Beyond Relativism and Objectivism: Science, Hermeneutics, and Praxis. Philadelphia: University of Pennsylvania Press.

Bernstein R.J., (1986), Philosophical Profiles. Philadelphia: University of Pennsylvania Press.

Bernstein R.J., (1991), New Constellation. Cambridge: MIT Press.

Birkhead, T. R., Johnson, S. D. & Nettleship, D. N. (1985). Extra-pair matings and mate guarding in the common murre Uria aalge. - Anim. Behav. 33, p. 608-619.

Beauregard, Mario, and Vincent Paquette. "Neural Correlates of a Mystical Experience in Carmelite Nuns." Neuroscience Letters 405, no. 3 (2006)

Benson, Herbert. Timeless Healing: The Power and Biology of Belief. New York: Scribner, 1996

Bose, Subhas Chandra. An Indian Pilgrim: An Unfinished Autobiography, Oxford University Press, 1997

Bogen, J.E.(1995a), 'On the neurophysiology of consciousness: Part I. An overview', Consciousness and Cognition, 4.

Bogen, J.E. (1995b), 'On the neurophysiology of consciousness: Part II. Constraining the semantic problem', Consciousness and Cognition, 4.

Bremner, J. D., R. Soufer, et al. (2001). "Gender differences in cognitive and neural correlates of remembrance of emotional words." Psychopharmacol Bull 35 (3).

Brothers, L. (2002). The social brain: A project for integrating primate behavior and neurophysiology in a new domain. In J. T. Cacioppo et al. (Eds.), Foundations in neuroscience. Cambridge, MA: MIT Press.

Buss, D. D. (2003). Evolutionary Psychology: The New Science of Mind, 2nd ed. New York: Allyn & Bacon.

Buss, D. M. (1989). "Conflict between the sexes: Strategic interference and the evocation of anger and upset." J Pers Soc Psychol 56 (5).

Buss, D. M. (1995). "Psychological sex differences. Origins through sexual selection." Am Psychol 50 (3).

Buss, D. M., and D. P. Schmitt (1993). "Sexual strategies theory: An evolutionary perspective on human mating." Psychol Rev 100 (2).

Blakemore SJ, Decety J (2001) From the perception of action to the understanding of intention. Nature Rev Neurosci 2: 561.

Colapietro V., (1988), "Human Agency: The Habits of Our Being." Southern Journal of Philosophy, XXVI, 2, pp. 153-68.

Colapietro V., (1992), "Purpose, Power, and Agency." The Monist, 75, 4 (October) pp. 423-44.

Colapietro V., (2004a), "C. S. Peirce's Reclamation of Teleology." Nature in American Philosophy, ed. Jean De Groot (Washington, D.C.: Catholic University Press of America), pp. 88-108.

Carey DP, Perrett DI, Oram MW (1997) Recognizing, understanding and reproducing actions. In: Jeannerod M, Grafman J (eds) Handbook of neuropsychology. Vol. 11: Action and cognition. Elsevier, Amsterdam.

Carr L, Iacoboni M, Dubeau MC, Mazziotta JC, Lenzi GL (2003) Neural mechanisms of empathy in humans: a relay from neural systems for imitation to limbic areas. Proc Natl Acad Sci USA 100: 5497–5502.

Chomsky Noam, (2017) Requiem for the American Dream

Chomsky Noam, (2016) Who Rules the World?

Chomsky Noam, (2010) How the World Works

Churchland, P.S. (1986), Neurophilosophy (Cambridge, MA: The MIT Press).

Churchland, P.S. & Ramachandran, V.S. (1993), 'Filling in: Why Dennett is wrong', in Dennett and His Critics: Demystifying Mind, ed. B. Dahlbom (Oxford: Blackwell Scientific Press).

Churchland, P.S., Ramachandran, V.S. & Sejnowski, T.J. (1994), 'A critique of pure vision', in Large- scale Neuronal Theories of the Brain, ed. C. Koch & J.L. Davis (Cambridge, MA: The MIT Press).

Coyle EF. Integration of the physiological factors determining endurance performance ability. Exerc Sport Sci Rev. 1995;23:25–63.

Crick, F. (1994), The Astonishing Hypothesis: The Scientific Search for the Soul (New York: Simon and Schuster).

Crick, F. (1996), 'Visual perception: rivalry and consciousness', Nature, 379.

Crick, F. & Koch, C. (1992), 'The problem of consciousness', Scientific American, 267.

Damasio, A (2003a) Looking for Spinoza. Harcourt Inc. Damasio A (2003b) Feeling of emotion and the self. Ann NY Acad Sci 1001: 253–261.

d'Aquili, Eugene. "Senses of Reality in Science and Religion." Zygon 17, no 4 (1982)

d'Aquili, Eugene. "The Biopsychological Determinants of Religious Ritual Behavior." Zygon 10, no. 1 (1975)

d'Aquili, Eugene. "The Myth-Ritual Complex: A Biogenetic Structural Analysis." Zygon 18, no. 3 (1983)

d'Aquili, Eugene, and Andrew Newberg. The Mystical Mind: Probing the Biology of Religious Experience. Minneapolis: Fortress Press, 1999.

Daly DD. 1958. Ictal affect. Am J Psychiatry.

Damasio, A. (1994) Descartes' Error: Emotion, Reason and the Human Brain. New York, Putnams.

Damasio, A. (1999) The Feeling of What Happens: Body, Emotion and the Making of Consciousness. London, Heinemann.

Darwin, C. (1859) On the Origin of Species by Means of Natural Selection. London, Murray.

Darwin, C. (1871) The Descent of Man and Selection in Relation to Sex. London, John Murray.

Darwin, C. (1872) The Expression of the Emotions in Man and Animals. London, John Murray; also published 1965, Chicago, University of Chicago Press.

Dawkins, M.S. (1987) Minding and mattering. In C. Blakemore and S. Greenfield (eds) Mindwaves. Oxford, Blackwell, 151-60.

Dawkins, R. (1976) The Selfish Gene. Oxford, Oxford University Press; a new edition, with additional material, was published in 1989.

Di Pellegrino G, Fadiga L, Fogassi L, Gallese V, Rizzolatti G (1992) Understanding motor events: A neurophysiological study. Exp Brain Res 91: 176–80.

Deikman, A.J. (2000) A functional approach to mysticism. Journal of Consciousness Studies 7(11-12), 75-91.

Delmonte, M.M. (1987) Personality and meditation. In M. West (ed.) The Psychology of Meditation. Oxford, Clarendon Press, 118-32.

Dennett, D.C. (1988) Quining qualia. In A.J. Marcel and E. Bisiach (eds) Consciousness in Contemporary Science. Oxford, Oxford University Press, 42-77.

Dennett, D.C. (1991) Consciousness Explained. Boston, MA, and London, Little, Brown and Co.

Dennett, D.C. (1995a) Darwin's Dangerous Idea. London, Penguin.

Dennett, D.C. (1998b) Brainchildren: Essays on Designing Minds. Cambridge, MA, MIT Press.

Dewhurst, Kenneth, and A. W. Beard. "Sudden Religious Conversions in Temporal Lobe Epilepsy." British Journal of Psychiatry 117 (1970)

Dewhurst K, Beard AW. Sudden religious conversions in temporal lobe epilepsy. 1970 Epilepsy Behav 2003

Devinsky O, Lai G. Spirituality and religion in epilepsy. Epilepsy Behav 2008.

Devinsky, O., Morrell, MJ, Vogt, BA. (1995) 'Contribution of anterior cingulate cortex to behavior', Brain, 118.

E. Horvitz, "One Hundred Year Study on Artificial Intelligence: Reflections and Framing," ed: Stanford University, 2014.

Eckhart Meister, Selected Writings

Egidi R., ed. (1999), "Von Wright and 'Dante's Dream': Stages in a Philosophical Pilgrim's Progress", in

In Search of a New Humanism: the Philosophy of G.H. von Wright, ed. by R. Egidi, Kluwer, Dordrecht.

Fadiga L, Fogassi L, Pavesi G, Rizzolatti G (1995) Motor facilitation during action observation: a magnetic stimulation study. J Neurophysiol 73: 2608–2611.

Fogassi L, Gallese V, Fadiga L, Rizzolatti G (1998) Neurons responding to the sight of goal directed hand/arm actions in the parietal area PF (7b) of the macaque monkey. Soc Neurosci Abs 24:257.5.

Frith U, Frith CD (2003) Development and neurophysiology of mentalizing. Philos Trans R Soc Lond B Biol Sci 358: 459.

Farah, M.J. (1989), 'The neural basis of mental imagery', Trends in Neurosciences, 10.

Finlay BL, Darlington RB (1995) Linked regularities in the development and evolution of mammalian brains. Science 268.

Freud, S. "The Interpretation of Dreams", 1900

Freud, S. "Selected papers on hysteria and other psychoneuroses" Journal of Nervous and Mental Disease 1909.

Freud, S. "The Origin and Development of Psychoanalysis", 1910

Freud, S. "Psychopathology of everyday life", 1914

Freud, S. "Beyond the Pleasure Principle", 1920

Frith, C.D. & Dolan, R.J. (1997), 'Abnormal beliefs: Delusions and memory', Paper presented at the May, 1997, Harvard Conference on Memory and Belief.

Gay, Volney, ed. Neuroscience and Religion. Plymouth, UK: Lexington Books, 2009.

Gazzaniga, M. S. (1985). The social brain. New York: Basic Books.

Gazzaniga, M.S. (1993), 'Brain mechanisms and conscious experience', Ciba Foundation Symposium, 174.

Geschwind N. "Behavioural changes in temporal lobe epilepsy". Psychol Med. 1979.

Gellhorn, E., Kiely, W.F. "Mystical states of consciousness: neurophysiological and clinical aspects." J Nerv Ment Dis. 1972;154:399-405.

Gilbert SL, Dobyns WB, Lahn BT (2005) Genetic links between brain development and brain evolution. Nat Rev Genet 6.

Gray JA. The Psychology of Fear and Stress. 2nd ed. New York, NY: Cambridge University Press; 1988.

Gloor, P. (1992), 'Amygdala and temporal lobe epilepsy', in The Amygdala: Neurobiological Aspects of Emotion, Memory and Mental Dysfunction, ed J.P. Aggleton (New York: Wiley-Liss).

Greenspan, S. I. and S. G. Shanker (2004). The first idea: How symbols, language, and intelligence evolved from our early primate ancestors to modern humans. Cambridge, MA: Da Capo Press.

Grady, D. (1993), 'The vision thing: Mainly in the brain', Discover, June.

Gallagher HL, Frith CD (2003) Functional imaging of 'theory of mind'. Trends Cogn Sci 7: 77.

Gallese V, Fogassi L, Fadiga L, Rizzolatti G (2002) Action representation and the inferior parietal lobule. In: Prinz W, Hommel B (eds) Attention & Performance XIX. Common mechanisms in perception and action. Oxford University Press, Oxford.

Gallese V, Keysers C, Rizzolatti G (2004) A unifying view of the basis of social cognition. Trends Cogn Sci 8: 396–403.

Goldman AI, Sripada CS (2004) Simulationist models of face-based emotion recognition. Cognition 94: 193–213.

Grèzes J, Costes N, Decety J (1998) Top-down effect of strategy on the perception of human biological motion: a PET investigation. Cogn Neuropsychol 15: 553–582.

Grèzes J, Armony JL, Rowe J, Passingham RE (2003) Activations related to "mirror" and "canonical" neurones in the human brain: an fMRI study. Neuroimage 18: 928–937.

Gross CG, Rocha-Miranda CE, Bender DB (1972) Visual properties of neurons in the inferotemporal cortex of the macaque. J Neurophysiol 35: 96–111.

Guevara Che, The Motorcycle Diaries, 1992

Hari R, Forss N, Avikainen S, Kirveskari S, Salenius S, Rizzolatti G (1998) Activation of human primary motor cortex during action observation: a neuromagnetic study. Proc. Natl Acad Sci USA 95: 15061–15065.

Hardy, G. H. (1940). Ramanujan. Cambridge: Cambridge University Press.

Hall, Daniel, Keith Meador, and Harold Koenig. "Measuring Religiousness in Health Research: Review and Critique." Journal of Religion and Health 47, no. 2 (2008)

Harris, Sam, Jonas Kaplan, Ashley Curiel, Susan Bookheimer, Marco Iacoboni, and Mark Cohen. "The Neural Correlates of Religious and

Nonreligious Belief." PLoS One 4, no. 10 (October 1, 2009)

Halgren, E. (1992), 'Emotional neurophysiology of the amygdala within the context of human cognition', in The Amygdala: Neurobiological Aspects of Emotion, Memory and Mental Dysfunction, ed J.P. Aggleton (New York: Wiley-Liss).

Halligan PW, Fink GR, Marshal JC, Vallar G. 2003. Spatial cognition: evidence from visual neglect. Trends Cogn Sci.

Handbook of Emotions, Edited by Michael Lewis, Jeannette M. Haviland-Jones, and Lisa Feldman Barrett, The Guilford Press; 3rd edition (2010).

Hameroff, S.R. and Penrose, R. (1996) Conscious events as orchestrated space-time selections. Journal of Consciousness Studies 3(1), 36-53; also reprinted in J. Shear (ed.) (1997) Explaining Consciousness-The Hard

Problem. Cambridge, MA, MIT Press, 177-95.

Harding, D.E. (1961) On Having no Head: Zen and the Re-Discovery of the Obvious. London, Buddhist Society.

Hardy, A. (1979) The Spiritual Nature of Man: A Study of Contemporary Religious Experience. Oxford, Clarendon Press.

Harre, R. and Gillett, G. (1994) The Discursive Mind. Thousand Oaks, CA, Sage.

Haugeland, J. (ed.) (1997) Mind Design II: Philosophy, Psychology, Artificial Intelligence. Cambridge, MA, MIT Press.

Hauser, M.D. (2000) Wild Minds: What Animals Really Think. New York, Henry Holt and Co.; London, Penguin.

Hebb, D.O. (1949) The Organization of Behavior. New York, Wiley.

Helmholtz, H.L.F. von (1856-67) Treatise on Physiological Optics.

Hess, EH (1975) "The role of pupil size in communication," Scientific American, 233(5), 110–12.

Heyes, C.M. (1998) Theory of mind in nonhuman primates. Behavioral and Brain Sciences 21, 101-48; with commentaries.

Heyes, C.M. and Galef, B.G. (eds) (1996) Social Learning in Animals: The Roots of Culture. San Diego, CA, Academic Press.

Hilgard, E.R. (1986) Divided Consciousness: Multiple Controls in Human Thought and Action. New York, Wiley.

Hilton, E.N., Lundberg, T.R. Transgender Women in the Female Category of Sport: Perspectives on Testosterone Suppression and Performance Advantage. Sports Med 51, 199–214 (2021).

Hitler, Adolf. Mein Kampf, 1925

Hodgson, R. (1891) A case of double consciousness. Proceedings of the Society for Psychical Research 7, 221-58.

Hofstadter, D.R. and Dennett, D.C. (eds) (1981) The Mind's I: Fantasies and Reflections on Self and Soul. London, Penguin.

Holland, J. (ed.) (2001) Ecstasy: The Complete Guide: A Comprehensive Look at the Risks and Benefits of MDMA. Rochester, VT, Park Street Press.

Holmes, D.S. (1987) The influence of meditation versus rest on physiological arousal. In M. West (ed.) The Psychology of Meditation. Oxford, Clarendon Press, 81-103.

Holmstrom, David. 1992, Christian Science Monitor

Holt, J. (1999) Blindsight in debates about qualia. Journal of Consciousness Studies 6(5), 54-71.

Holloway RL (1996) Evolution of the human brain. In: Lock A, Peters CR (eds) Handbook of human symbolic evolution. Oxford University Press, Oxford

Iacoboni M, Woods RP, Brass M, Bekkering H, Mazziotta JC, Rizzolatti G (1999) Cortical mechanisms of human imitation. Science 286: 2526–2528.

Iacoboni M, Koski LM, Brass M, Bekkering H, Woods RP, Dubeau MC, Mazziotta JC, Rizzolatti G (2001) Reafferent copies of imitated actions in the right superior temporal cortex. Proc Natl Acad Sci USA 98: 13995–13999.

Jeannerod M (1988) The neural and behavioural organization of goal-directed movements. Clarendon Press, Oxford.

Johnson-Frey SH, Maloof FR, Newman-Norlund R, Farrer C, Inati S, Grafton ST (2003) Actions or hand-objects interactions? Human inferior frontal cortex and action observation. Neuron 39: 1053–1058.

Jackson, F. (1982) Epiphenomenal qualia. Philosophical Quarterly 32, 127-36.

James, W. (1890) The Principles of Psychology (2 volumes). London, Macmillan.

James, W. (1902) The Varieties of Religious Experience: A Study in Human Nature. New York and London, Longmans, Green and Co.

Jansen, K. (2001) Ketamine: Dreams and Realities. Sarasota, FL, Multidisciplinary Association for Psychedelic Studies.

Jay, M. (ed.) (1999) Artificial Paradises: A Drugs Reader. London, Penguin.

Jaynes, J. (1976) The Origin of Consciousness in the Breakdown of the Bicameral Mind. New York, Houghton Mifflin.

Johnson, M.K. and Raye, C.L. (1981) Reality monitoring. Psychological Review 88, 67-85.

Kadim I, Mahgoub O, Baqir S et al. (2015) Cultured meat from muscle stem cells: a review of challenges and prospects. J Integr Agr 14: 222–233

Kandel, E. R. In Search of Memory: The Emergence of a New Science of Mind, W. W. Norton & Company (2007).

Kandel E. R. Schwartz JH, Jessel TM. Principles of neural sciences. New York; McGraw Hill, 2000.

Kanwisher, N. (2001) Neural events and perceptual awareness. Cognition

79, 89-113; also reprinted inS. Dehaene (ed.) The Cognitive Neuroscience of Consciousness. Cambridge, MA, MIT Press, 89-113.

Karn, K. and Hayhoe, M. (2000) Memory representations guide targeting eye movements in a natural task. Visual Cognition 7, 673-703.

Kennedy, H., & Dehay, C. (1988). Functional implications of the anatomical organization of the callosal projections of visual areas V1 and V2 in the macaque monkey. Behav. Brain Res., 29, 225–236.

Kentridge, R.W. and Heywood, C.A. (1999) The status of blindsight. Journal of Consciousness Studies 6(5), 3-11.

Kihlstrom, J.F. (1996) Perception without awareness of what is perceived, learning without awareness of what is learned. In M. Velmans (ed.) The Science of Consciousness. London, Routledge, 23-46.

Kosslyn, S.M. (1980) Image and Mind. Cambridge, MA, Harvard University Press.

Kosslyn, S.M. (1988) Aspects of a cognitive neuroscience of mental imagery. Science 240, 1621-6.

Kinsbourne, M. (1995), 'The intralaminar thalamic nucleii', Consciousness and Cognition, 4.

Kjaer, Troels, Camilla Bertelsen, Paola Piccini, David Brooks, Jorgen Alving, and Hans Lou. "Increased Dopamine Tone during Meditation- Induced Change of Consciousness." Cognitive Brain Research 13, no. 2 (April 2002)

Kölmel HW. 1985. Complex visual hallucinations in the hemianopic field. J Neurol Neurosurg Psychiatry.

Koenig, Harold. "Research on Religion, Spirituality, and Mental Health: A Review." Canadian Journal of Psychiatry 54, no. 5 (May 2009)

Koenig, Harold, ed. Handbook of Religion and Mental Health. San Diego, CA: Academic Press, 1998

Kraepelin E. Psychiatry: A Textbook for Students and Physicians. New York, NY: Science History Publications; 1990.

Lauglin, Charles, John McManus, and Eugene d'Aquili. Brain, Symbol, and Experience. 2nd ed. New York: Columbia University Press, 1992

Lakoff, G. and M. Johnson (1999). Philosophy in the flesh. Basic Books: New York.

LeDoux, J. E. (1996). The emotional brain. New York: Simon & Schuster.

LeDoux, J.E. (1992), 'Emotion and the amygdala', in The Amygdala: Neurobiological Aspects of Emo- tion, Memory and Mental Dysfunction, ed J.P. Aggleton (New York: Wiley-Liss).

Levin, D.T. and Simons, D.J. (1997) Failure to detect changes to attended objects in motion pictures. Psychonomic Bulletin and Review 4, 501-6.

Levine,J. (1983) Materialism and qualia: the explanatory gap. Pacific Philosophical Quarterly 64, 354-61.

Levine,J. (2001) Purple Haze: The Puzzle of Consciousness. New York, Oxford University Press. Levine, S. (1979) A Gradual Awakening. New York, Doubleday.

Levinson, B.W. (1965) States of awareness during general anaesthesia. British Journal of Anaesthesia 37, 544-6.

Lewicki, P., Czyzewska, M. and Hoffman, H. (1987) Unconscious acquisition of complex procedural knowledge. Journal of Experimental Psychology: Learning, Memory and Cognition 13, 523-30.

Lewicki, P., Hill, T. and Bizot, E. (1988) Acquisition of procedural knowledge about a pattern of stimuli that cannot be articulated. Cognitive Psychology 20, 24-37.

Lewicki, P., Hill, T. and Czyzewska, M. (1992) Nonconscious acquisition of information. American Psychologist 47, 796-801.

Manthey S, Schubotz RI, von Cramon DY (2003). Premotor cortex in observing erroneous action: an fMRI study. Brain Res Cogn Brain Res 15: 296–307.

Mesulam MM, Mufson EJ (1982) Insula of the old world monkey. III: Efferent cortical output and comments on function. J Comp Neurol 212: 38–52.

Naskar, Abhijit. "Homo: A Brief History of Consciousness", 2015

Naskar, Abhijit. "What is Mind?", 2016

Naskar, Abhijit. "Love, God & Neurons: Memoir of A Scientist who found himself by getting lost", 2016

Naskar, Abhijit. "Principia Humanitas", 2017

Naskar, Abhijit. "We Are All Black: A Treatise on Racism", 2017

Naskar, Abhijit. "Either Civilized or Phobic: A Treatise on Homosexuality", 2017

Naskar, Abhijit. "The Bengal Tigress: A Treatise on Gender Equality", 2017

Naskar, Abhijit. "Morality Absolute", 2017

Naskar, Abhijit. "Build Bridges not Walls: In the name of Americana", 2018

Naskar, Abhijit. "Fabric of Humanity", 2018

Naskar, Abhijit. "Citizens of Peace: Beyond the Savagery of Sovereignty", 2019

Naskar, Abhijit. "The Constitution of The United Peoples of Earth", 2019

Naskar, Abhijit. "Neurons Giveth, Neurons Taketh Away | Abhijit Naskar | TEDxIIMRanchi", 2019 https://www.youtube.com/watch?v=B NX-Q0ySm80

Naskar, Abhijit. "Mission Reality", 2019

Naskar, Abhijit. "Operation Justice: To Make A Society That Needs No Law", 2019

Naskar, Abhijit. "Every Generation Needs Caretakers: The Gospel of Patriotism", 2020

Naskar, Abhijit. "Hurricane Humans: Give me accountability, I'll give you peace", 2020

Naskar, Abhijit. "Revolution Indomable", 2020

Naskar, Abhijit. "Servitude is Sanctitude", 2020

Naskar, Abhijit. "Good Scientist: When Science and Service Combine", 2020

Newberg, Andrew, and Jeremy Iversen. "The Neural Basis of the Complex Mental Task of Meditation: Neurotransmitter and Neurochemical Considerations." Medical Hypotheses 61, no. 2 (2003).

Newberg, Andrew. "How God Changes Your Brain: An Introduction to Jewish Neurotheology", CCAR Journal: The Reform Jewish Quarterly, Winter 2016.

Newberg, Andrew, and Stephanie Newberg. "A Neuropsychological Perspective on Spiritual Development." In Handbook of Spiritual Development in Childhood and Adolescence, edited by Eugene

Roehlkepartain, Pamela King, Linda Wagener, and Peter Benson. London: Sage Publications, Inc., 2005

Newberg, Andrew. "The Neurotheology Link An Intersection Between Spirituality and Health", Alternative and Complimentary Therapies, Vol 21 No 1, February 2015.

Newberg, Andrew, Nancy Wintering, Dharma Khalsa, Hannah Roggenkamp, and Mark Waldman. "Meditation Effects on Cognitive Function and Cerebral Blood Flow in Subjects with Memory Loss: A Preliminary Study." Journal of Alzheimer's Disease 20, no. 2 (2010)

Nash, M. (1995), 'Glimpses of the mind', Time.

Nesse RM. Proximate and evolutionary studies of anxiety, stress and depression: synergy at the interface. Neurosci Biobehav Rev. 1999;23:895-903.

Nicolelis, Miguel. (2011) "Beyond Boundaries: The New Neuroscience of Connecting Brains with Machines---and How It Will Change Our Lives", Times Books

O'Hara, K. and Scutt, T. (1996) There is no hard problem of consciousness. Journal of Consciousness Studies 3(4), 290-302, reprinted in J. Shear (ed.) (1997) Explaining Consciousness. Cambridge, MA, MIT Press, 69-82.

O'Regan, J.K. (1992) Solving the "real" mysteries of visual perception: the world as an outside memory. Canadian Journal of Psychology 46, 461-88.

O'Regan, J.K. and Noe, A. (2001) A sensorimotor account of vision and visual consciousness. Behavioral and Brain Sciences 24(5), 883-917.

O'Regan, J.K., Rensink, R.A. and Clark,].]. (1999) Change-blindness as a result of "mudsplashes." Nature 398, 34.

Ornstein, R.E. (1977) The Psychology of Consciousness (2nd edn). New York, Harcourt.

Ornstein, R.E. (1986) The Psychology of Consciousness (3rd edn). New York, Pehguin.

Ornstein, R.E. (1992) The Evolution of Consciousness. New York, Touchstone.

Penfield W, Faulk ME (1955) The insula: further observations on its function. Brain 78: 445– 470.

Penrose, R. (1994), Shadows of the Mind (Oxford: Oxford University Press).

Penrose, R. (1989), The Emperor's New Mind: Concerning Computers, Minds and The Laws of Physics (Oxford: Oxford University Press).

Persinger, "'I would kill in God's name' role of sex, weekly church attendance, report of a religious experience and limbic lability" Perceptual and Motor Skills 1997.

Persinger "Experimental simulation of the God experience" Neurotheology 2003.

Persinger, Corradini, Clement, Keaney, et al "Neurotheology and its convergence with neuroquantology" NeuroQuantology 2010.

Persinger, Koren and St-Pierre "The electromagnetic induction of mystical and altered states within the laboratory" Journal of Consciousness Exploration and Research 2010.

Persinger "Case report: A prototypical spontaneous 'sensed presence' of a sentient being and concomitant electroencephalographic activity in the clinical laboratory" Neurocase 2008.

Persinger and Saroka "Potential production of Hughlings Jackson's "parasitic consciousness" by physiologically-patterned weak transcerebral magnetic fields: QEEG and source localization" Epilepsy & Behavior 28 (2013).

Persinger. "The neuropsychiatry of paranormal experiences". J Neuropsychiatry Clin Neurosci 2001.

Persinger. "Neuropsychological bases of god beliefs", New York: Praeger, 1987

Persinger. "Temporal lobe epileptic signs and correlative behaviors displayed by normal populations", Journal of General Psychology, 1986

Perry BD, Pollard R. Homeostasis, stress, trauma, and adaptation. A neurodevelopmental view of childhood trauma. Child Adolesc Psychiatr Clin N Am. 1998;7:33.

Paré, D. & Llinás, R. (1995), 'Conscious and preconscious processes as seen from the standpoint of sleep-waking cycle neurophysiology', Neuropsychologia, 33.

Phillips ML, Young AW, Senior C, Brammer M, Andrew C, Calder AJ, Bullmore ET, Perrett DI, Rowland D, Williams SC, Gray JA, David AS (1997) A specific neural substrate for perceiving facial expressions of disgust. Nature 389: 495–498.

Phillips ML, Young AW, Scott SK, Calder AJ, Andrew C, Giampietro V, Williams SC, Bullmore ET, Brammer M, Gray JA (1998) Neural responses to facial and vocal expressions of fear and disgust. Proc R Soc Lond B Biol Sci 265: 1809–1817.

Puce A, Perrett D (2003) Electrophysiological and brain imaging of biological motion. Philosoph Trans Royal Soc Lond, Series B, 358: 435–445.

Ramachandran VS. Behavioral and magnetoencephalographic correlates of plasticity in the adult human brain. Proc Natl Acad Sci USA 1993; 90: 10413–20.

Ramachandran VS. Phantom limbs, neglect syndromes, repressed memories, and Freudian psychology. Int Rev Neurobiol 1994; 37: 291–333.

Ramachandran VS. Plasticity and functional recovery in neurology. Clin Med 2005; 5: 368–73.

Ramachandran VS, Hirstein W. The perception of phantom limbs. The D. O. Hebb lecture. Brain 1998; 121: 1603–30.

Ramachandran VS, Rogers-Ramachandran D, Cobb S. Touching the phantom limb. Nature 1995; 377: 489–90.

Ramachandran VS, Rogers-Ramachandran D. Phantom limbs and

neural plasticity. Arch Neurol 2000; 57: 317–20.

Ramachandran VS, Rogers-Ramachandran D. It's all done with mirrors. Sci Am Mind 2007; 18: 16–9.

Ramachandran VS, Rogers-Ramachandran D. Sensations referred to a patient's phantom arm from another subjects intact arm: perceptual correlates of mirror neurons. Med Hypotheses 2008; 70: 1233–4.

Ramachandran VS, Rogers-Ramachandran D, Stewart M. Perceptual correlates of massive cortical reorganization. Science 1992; 258: 1159–60.

Rizzolatti G, Craighero L (2004) The mirror-neuron system. Annu Rev Neurosci 27: 169–192.

Rizzolatti G, Fogassi L, Gallese V (2001) Neurophysiological mechanisms underlying the understanding and imitation of action. Nature Rev Neurosci 2:661–670.

Rock I, Victor J. Vision and touch: an experimentally created conflict between the two senses. Science 1964; 143: 594–6.

Rose'n B, Lundborg G. Training with a mirror in rehabilitation of the hand. Scand J Plast Reconstr Surg Hand Surg 2005; 39: 104–8.

Roberts, TA; Smalley, J; Ahrendt, D (December 2020). "Effect of gender affirming hormones on athletic performance in transwomen and transmen: implications for sporting organisations and legislators". British Journal of Sports Medicine. 55 (11): 577–583

Royet JP, Plailly J, Delon-Martin C, Kareken DA, Segebarth C (2003) fMRI of emotional responses to odors: influence of hedonic valence and judgment, handedness, and gender. Neuroimage 20: 713–728.

Rozin R Haidt J and McCauley CR (2000) Disgust. In: Lewis M, Haviland-Jones JM (eds) Handbook of Emotion. 2nd Edition. Guilford Press, New York, pp 637–653.

Saxe R, Carey S, Kanwisher N (2004) Understanding other minds: linking developmental psychology and functional neuroimaging. Annu Rev Psychol 55: 87–124.

S. J. Russell and P. Norvig, Artificial intelligence: a modern approach (3rd edition): Prentice Hall, 2009.

Singer T, Seymour B, O'Doherty J, Kaube H, Dolan RJ, Frith CD (2004) Empathy for pain involves the affective but not the sensory components of pain. Science 303: 1157–1162.

Smith A (1759) The theory of moral sentiments (ed. 1976). Clarendon Press, Oxford.

Schilling, Vincent. 2017, indian country today

Stein, Stephen K. 2017, The Sea in World History: Exploration, Travel, and Trade

Simonsen R (2015) Eating for the future: veganism and the challenge of in vitro meat. In: Stapleton P, Byers A (Hg). Biopolitics and utopia. Palgrave Macmillan, New York (2015), S 167–190

Tesla N. "My Inventions", 1919

T. R. Society, "Machine learning: the power and promise of computers that learn by example," ed. The Royal Society, 2017.

Tomasello M, Call J (1997) Primate cognition. Oxford University Press, Oxford.